DATE DUE

Community Helpers

Truck Drivers

by Erika S. Manley

FX: 04-18

Bullfrog Books

Ideas for Parents and Teachers

Bullfrog Books let children practice reading informational text at the earliest reading levels. Repetition, familiar words, and photo labels support early readers.

Before Reading

- Discuss the cover photo. What does it tell them?

- Look at the picture glossary together. Read and discuss the words.

Read the Book

- "Walk" through the book and look at the photos. Let the child ask questions. Point out the photo labels.

- Read the book to the child, or have him or her read independently.

After Reading

- Prompt the child to think more. Ask: Do you know anyone who drives a truck for a living? What sorts of things does he or she transport?

Bullfrog Books are published by Jump!
5357 Penn Avenue South
Minneapolis, MN 55419
www.jumplibrary.com

Library of Congress Cataloging-in-Publication Data

Names: Manley, Erika S., author.
Title: Truck drivers / by Erika S. Manley.
Description: Minneapolis, MN: Jump!, Inc., [2017]
Series: Community helpers | Audience: Age 5–8.
Audience: K to grade 3. | Includes index.
Identifiers: LCCN 2016052582 (print)
LCCN 2017007013 (ebook) | ISBN 9781620316757
(hardcover: alk. paper) | ISBN 9781620317280 (pbk.)
ISBN 9781624965524 (ebook)
Subjects: LCSH: Truck driving—Juvenile literature.
Classification: LCC TL230.3 .M34 2017 (print)
LCC TL230.3 (ebook) | DDC 629.28/44—dc23
LC record available at https://lccn.loc.gov/2016052582

Editor: Jenny Fretland VanVoorst
Book Designer: Leah Sanders
Photo Researcher: Leah Sanders

Photo Credits: cristovao/Shutterstock, cover; Michael Shake/Shutterstock, cover; Karl R. Martin/Shutterstock, 1; Lisa F. Young/Shutterstock, 3; marcduf/iStock, 4; Kzenon/Shutterstock, 5; Andyqwe/iStock, 6–7; Edwin Remsberg/age fotostock/SuperStock, 8; David Touchtone/Shutterstock, 9; Jetta Productions/Getty, 10–11, 12–13, 22; Krivosheev Vitaly/Shutterstock, 14–15; Chubykin Arkady/Shutterstock, 16–17; Baloncici/Dreamstime, 19; Lithiumphoto/Shutterstock, 19; ColorBlind Images/Getty, 20–21; Rob Hyrons/Shutterstock, 23.

Printed in the United States of America at Corporate Graphics in North Mankato, Minnesota.

Table of Contents

Long Haul

Sam wants to be a truck driver.

What do they do?

They drive big trucks.
They transport goods.

Meg hauls fruits and vegetables.

She picks them up at the farm.

She will deliver
them to a store.

Thad wants to be a truck driver, too.

First, he must take a test.

He studies for the test.

He learns to drive safely.

He passes the test.

Now he can drive a truck.

Yay!

Henry drives a semi.

He travels many miles every day.

It is late.

Henry takes a break.

He is far from home.

He calls his family
to say hi.

bed

Henry sleeps in his truck.

Time to get up.
Let's drive!

Truck drivers do good work!

In the Truck

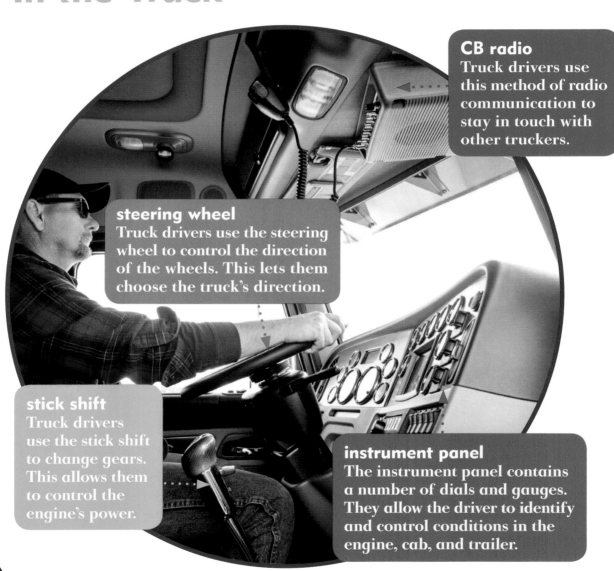

CB radio
Truck drivers use this method of radio communication to stay in touch with other truckers.

steering wheel
Truck drivers use the steering wheel to control the direction of the wheels. This lets them choose the truck's direction.

stick shift
Truck drivers use the stick shift to change gears. This allows them to control the engine's power.

instrument panel
The instrument panel contains a number of dials and gauges. They allow the driver to identify and control conditions in the engine, cab, and trailer.

Picture Glossary

deliver
To hand over.

semi
A trucking rig
made up of
a tractor and
a semitrailer.

goods
Items that have
been grown on
a farm, made
in a factory, or
crafted by hand.

transport
To move from
one place
to another.

Index

To Learn More

Learning more is as easy as 1, 2, 3.

1) Go to www.factsurfer.com

2) Enter "truckdrivers" into the search box.

3) Click the "Surf" button to see a list of websites.

With factsurfer.com, finding more information is just a click away.